A ROOKIE BIOGRAPHY

ROY CAMPANELLA

Major-League Champion

By Carol Greene

CHILDRENS PRESS ®

CHICAGO

This book is for Lloyd and LaVerne Wilson.

Roy Campanella (1921-1993)

Library of Congress Cataloging-in-Publication Data

Greene, Carol.
    Roy Campanella, major-league champion / by Carol Greene.
       p.   cm. — (A Rookie biography)
    Includes index. ISBN 0-516-04261-0
    1. Campanella, Roy, 1921-1993—Juvenile literature. 2. Baseball
players—United States—Biography—Juvenile literature. [1. Campanella,
Roy, 1921-1993. 2. Baseball players. 3. Afro-Americans—Biography.]
I. Title. II. Series: Greene, Carol. Rookie biography.
GV865.C3G74   1994
796.357′092—dc20
[B]   93-37878
                                           CIP
                                           AC

Roy Campanella
was a real person.
He was born in 1921.
He died in 1993.
Roy was one of the first
black baseball players
in the major leagues.
He was also a great man.
This is his story.

TABLE OF CONTENTS

E. Gaston Dobson

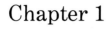

Chapter 1

That Crazy Game

The ball was old.
The bats were cracked.
Young Roy and his friends
in Philadelphia didn't care.
They were playing baseball.

Roy couldn't see well
through the big catcher's mask.
So he took it off.
Then Tommy fouled a pitch.
The ball hit Roy's nose.
Smack! Blood was all over.

"What happened?"
asked his dad at supper.

Roy told him.
"It doesn't hurt much," he said.
"I'll wear a mask tomorrow."

"What do you mean?" yelled his dad.
"Do you think you're going to
play that crazy game again?"

He made Roy promise
not to play baseball again.
Most of the time,
Roy obeyed his parents.
They were strict with
all four Campanella kids.

But Roy couldn't keep that promise.
He *had* to play baseball.

He had pictures of players
on the walls of his room.
He listened to games on the radio.
He watched big-league games
from a rooftop.

Once Roy went to a game
and tried to grab
a home-run ball.
He fell out of the stands
and hurt his wrist.

"All that and you didn't even
get the ball?" asked his dad.
He was almost laughing.

Roy didn't do well in school.
His mind was full of baseball.
But he worked in other ways.

He got up at 2 A.M.
and delivered milk
in a horse-drawn wagon.
He sold newspapers.
He shined shoes.
Roy liked to earn money.

Roy's dad was white.
His mother was black.
Sometimes kids called
Roy "halfbreed."

But as soon as it
was time for baseball,
the kids forgot about race.
They all played together.

And Roy Campanella
thought baseball was
"the onliest sport there is."
Promise or no promise,
he had to play
that crazy game.

The Bacharach Giants team in the year 1920

Chapter 2

A Great Start

In his early teens, Roy
played on neighborhood teams.
Then he played on
an American Legion team.
People began to see
how well he played.

When Roy was 15,
Tom Dixon asked him to play
for the Bacharach Giants,
a black semi-pro team.
Back then, black players
and white players
were on separate teams.

Biz Mackey was a star in the Negro National League.

Mr. Dixon told Roy's mother
that Roy could play
and go to school too.
So, all at once, Roy
became a real catcher.
The guys called him "Campy."

But Roy didn't stay with
that team for long.
Soon Biz Mackey asked
him to catch for the
Baltimore Elite Giants.
They were a professional team
in the Negro National League.

That summer, Roy traveled
with the Elite Giants.
Biz Mackey taught him
a lot about catching.

Roy Campanella (right) and Sammy Hughes
were teammates on the Elite Giants.

When school started again,
Roy's body was there.
But his heart wasn't.
At last his parents said
he could quit school
and play ball full-time.

On March 17, 1938,
Roy left for spring training
in Nashville, Tennessee.
His mother sent some food
and a Bible with him.

That was the start
of a good life for Roy.
During the regular season,
he played with the Elites.
In winter, he played
in Latin America.

Campanella in 1942, catching for the Elite Giants

Then one day in 1945,
a man called Branch Rickey
said he wanted to talk to Roy.

17

Jackie Robinson was the first black man
to play for a major-league baseball team.

Chapter 3

Dodger Days

Mr. Rickey was president
of the Brooklyn Dodgers.
He asked Roy to play for him.
But Roy thought Mr. Rickey
was starting a new black team.
He didn't want to play
on that team.

Then Jackie Robinson
told Roy that Mr. Rickey
meant the Brooklyn Dodgers.
Robinson had said yes.
Now he would be the first
black in the major leagues.

Roy felt bad.
He had missed his chance
to play in the major leagues.

But the next spring, Mr. Rickey
gave Roy another chance.
This time Roy said yes.
Soon he was on his way
to the Dodgers' farm club
in New Hampshire.

Roy Campanella meeting with Branch Rickey

Roy played
on the Dodgers'
farm teams in
New Hampshire
and in Montreal,
Canada.

The next year—1947—
Roy moved up to
the Dodgers' farm team
in Montreal, Canada.

21

Roy played his first major-league game for the Brooklyn Dodgers in 1948.

At last, on July 2, 1948,
Roy played for the big team—
the Brooklyn Dodgers.
He went to Ebbets Field,
put on uniform 39,
and stood by the batting cage.

"It was a sweet feeling,"
Roy said later.
He got three hits that night.

Safe! calls the umpire as Campanella slides into home plate
during a game against the Boston Braves in September 1949.

In 1949, Roy was catcher
for the whole All-Star game.
He did the same thing
in 1950, 1951, 1952, and 1953.
That was an All-Star record.

In 1949, Roy also got to
play in the World Series.
The Yankees beat the Dodgers,
but Roy played well.

Campanella tags out a runner at home plate
during the 1951 All-Star game.

Roy (standing at left) and Jackie Robinson (at right, with basketball) working with children at the Harlem YMCA.

When Roy wasn't playing,
he liked to help children.
He worked at the Harlem YMCA.
He spoke at schools
and held baseball clinics.

Roy also spent time at home with his wife Ruthie and their children. His hobbies were collecting tropical fish and electric trains.

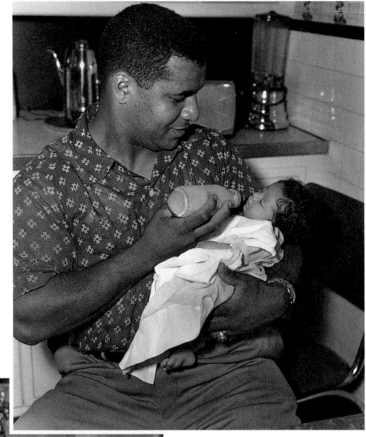

Roy at home in 1953, feeding his baby daughter (above) and working on his model railroad (left).

Roy proudly
shows off
the award
he won for
Most Valuable
Player in 1951.

Roy was chosen
Most Valuable Player
in the National League
in 1951, 1953, and 1955.

But he said that 1953 was
his best year in baseball.
He hit 42 home runs
and drove in 142 runs.
Still, he liked 1955 too, because
the Dodgers won the World Series.

Roy knew that when he was
too old to play ball,
he could become a coach
for the Dodgers.

And, starting in 1958,
the team would play
in Los Angeles, California.
That would be fun.

So life looked good to Roy
until early in the morning
of January 28, 1958.
"Then," he said, "the world
turned upside down for me."

Chapter 4

The Hardest Battle

Roy was driving home
that dark, snowy morning.
He was always a good driver.
But his car hit some ice and
crashed into a pole.

A policeman stands beside the car that Roy Campanella was driving
when it crashed into a pole (left). Campanella lies on a
stretcher (right) after being taken from the wrecked car.

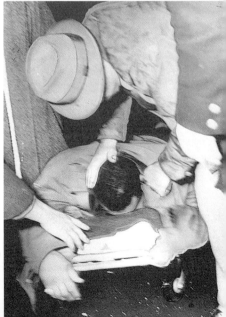

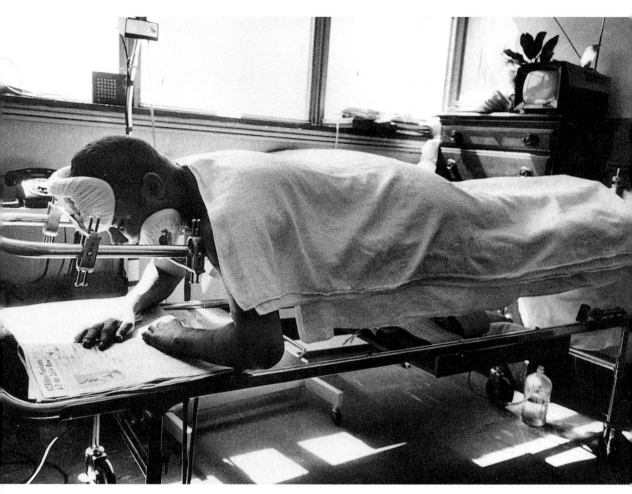

Roy reads the sports page while resting on
a specially designed bed in the hospital.

Roy's neck was broken.

His spinal column was hurt, too.

Doctors saved his life.

But Roy was paralyzed

from his chest down.

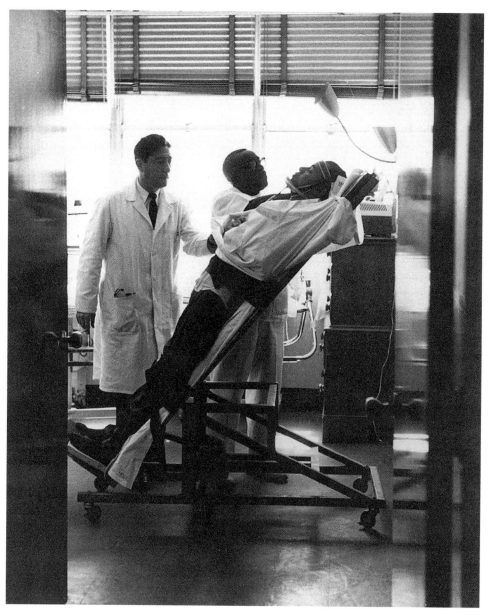

Four months after his accident, Roy was able to leave his bed. A tilt board held him in an upright position.

For a while, he lay
strapped to a bed.
He couldn't eat or drink
or do anything for himself.
Roy felt very sad
and very scared.

Then one day, he thought
about the Bible
his mother had given him.
He asked a nurse
to turn to Psalm 23.

"The Lord is my shepherd.
I shall not want . . ."

"From that moment on,"
said Roy later, "I knew
I was going to make it."

And he began to fight
the hardest battle of his life.

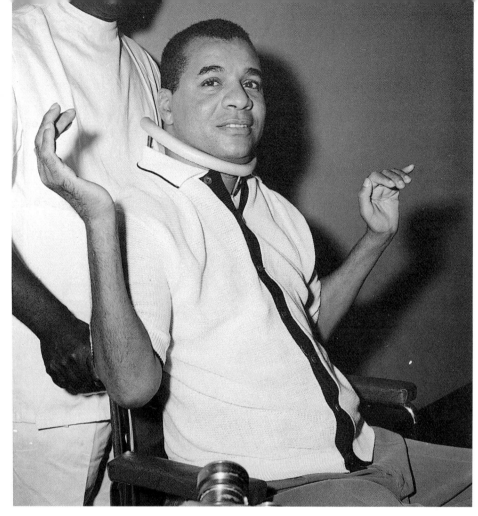

As he talks with reporters nine months after the accident, Roy shows that he can use his arms again.

He learned to sit up,
use his arms and hands
a little, feed himself,
and use a wheelchair.

Being with other patients
helped him feel better.
It helped them, too.

By September, Roy had
his own five-minute radio show
from the hospital.
Then he went to
a World Series game.
In November, he went home.

Roy with his family in November 1958

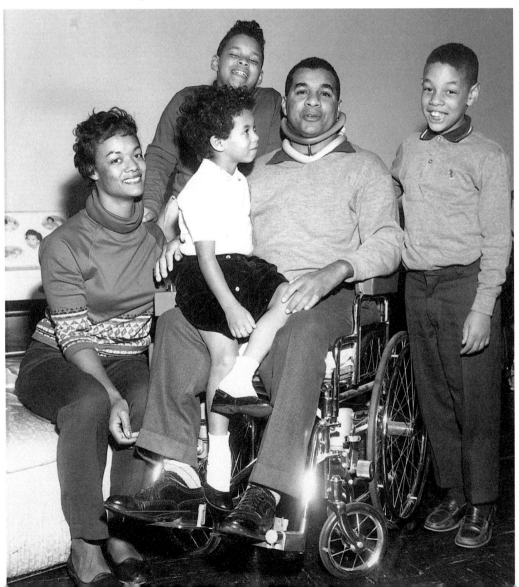

Campanella became a coach for the Dodgers. Here he
talks with Dodger catchers about the game.

By spring of 1959, Roy
was back with the Dodgers.
He couldn't play or even walk.
But he could help
young catchers and pitchers.
So he had a job.

On May 7, 1959,
93,103 people came to see
the Dodgers play the Yankees
in Los Angeles.
It was the largest crowd
in baseball history.

On May 7, 1959, a special game was held at Dodger Stadium to honor Roy Campanella.

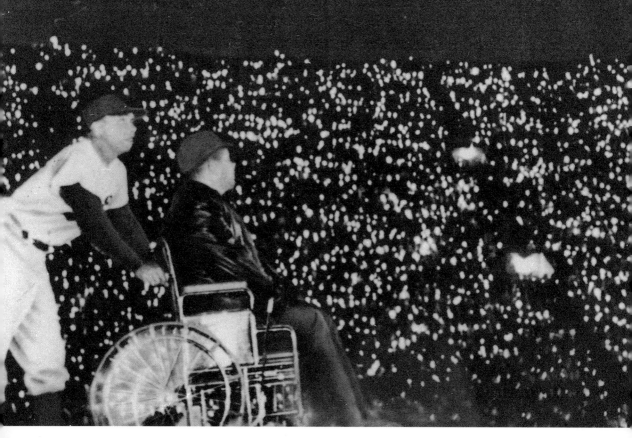

Roy watches from his wheelchair as 93,103 fans hold lighted matches.

The two teams were
playing a special game
to honor Roy.
In the fifth inning,
they turned out the lights
and each fan lit a match.

It was baseball's way
of telling Roy,
"We love you."

Right: Roy and Tommy Davis of the New York Mets conduct a clinic for young players in New York City. Below: Roy and Jackie Robinson with a copy of Robinson's book about the first black players in major-league baseball.

Chapter 5

A Full Life

Roy lived for 35 years
after his accident.
He never walked again,
and his body gave
him other problems.

Roy had family problems, too.
He and his wife Ruthie
broke up in 1960.

But Roy still loved life.
He made those years good.

In 1964, he married
an old friend, Roxie Doles.
She was a nurse
and could care for him.
She also loved life
—and Roy—a lot.

Roy was honored
at a special
dinner in 1978.
He is shown
here at the
dinner with his
wife Roxie
and baseball
commissioner
Bowie Kuhn.

Above: Roy and some young friends working to help paralyzed
people. Below: Roy talks with French jockey Claude de Leuze,
who was paralyzed when he fell from a horse.

Roy went on
helping
young players.
And he spent
much time
with other
paralyzed people.
He wanted them
all to live
a full life.

In 1969 Roy was photographed with his fellow Hall of Fame members.

In 1969, Roy was elected
to the Baseball Hall of Fame.
In 1978, he and his family
moved to Woodland Hills,
a suburb of Los Angeles.

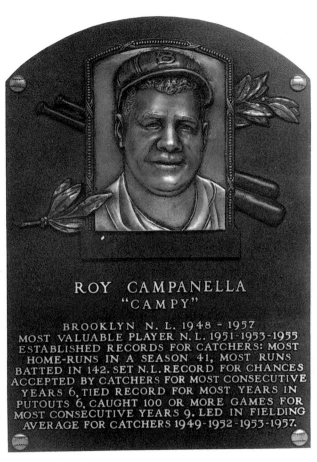

**Roy in 1989 (left). A plaque (right) is displayed
in the Hall of Fame to honor his baseball career.**

There, on June 26, 1993,
Roy died of a heart attack.
He was 71 years old.

Highlights from Roy's baseball career:
He crosses home plate after hitting
a home run, tags a runner out at
home (top), and works out before a game
at Ebbets Field (right).

Roy with Chuck Dressan and Jackie Robinson (above) at an Old Timers Game in 1962

Roy Campanella was
a great baseball player.
But he was an even greater man.
He was a champion.

"He makes you feel good
all over," said one fan.
"He just touches your life."

Important Dates

1921   November 19—Born in Philadelphia, Pennsylvania, to Ida and John Campanella

1937   Played with Bacharach Giants
Began play with Baltimore Elite Giants, Negro National League

1946   Signed with Brooklyn Dodgers; played at Nashua, New Hampshire

1947   Played at Montreal, Canada

1948   Began play with Brooklyn Dodgers

1951
1953   Chosen Most Valuable Player in the National League
1955

1958   Paralyzed from the chest down in an automobile accident

1959   Dodgers and Yankees played special game in his honor

1969   Inducted into Baseball Hall of Fame

1978   Moved to Woodland Hills, California

1993   June 26—Died in Woodland Hills

INDEX

Page numbers in boldface type indicate illustrations.

PHOTO CREDITS

ABOUT THE AUTHOR

Carol Greene has degrees in English literature and musicology. She has worked in international exchange programs, as an editor, and as a teacher of writing. She now lives in Webster Groves, Missouri, and writes full-time. She has published more than 100 books, including those in the Childrens Press Rookie Biographies series.